THE WOMB OF YOUR PRAYERS

THE *Womb* OF YOUR *Prayers*

BIRTHING GOD'S ANSWERS TO YOUR INTERCESSION

SYLVIA L. WILLIAMS

XULON PRESS

Xulon Press
2301 Lucien Way #415
Maitland, FL 32751
407.339.4217
www.xulonpress.com

P.O. Box 74494
Romulus, Mich. 48174
(734) 925-3257/ (313) 538-2930 fax
moregraceministries@aol.com

Paperback ISBN-13: 978-1-6628-2579-8
Ebook ISBN-13: 978-1-6628-2580-4

DEDICATION

This book is dedicated to my friend Laurence, and to my spiritual daughters, Valtina and Debra, who left me way too soon. To my mother, Joycie, who believed in me through thick and thin. Thank you for being a godly example and a woman of faith and prayer. Thank God for my siblings—Beatrice, Buster, Linda, Vincent, Darrell, and Robert. Your unwavering faith in me and encouragement over the years means more than you know. To my husband Lee, who has patiently stood beside me over the years, and in recent months, as I labored to birth this body of work. To my son Barry, who grew up with a praying mother who is also a minister. To my daughter Malaika, son-in-law Owen, and to their amazing children—you all are prayer in action. And what would I have done without my Women of Destiny and Grace, and Merciful Ministries families? Your love and prayers have been a constant source of inspiration.

Table of Contents

Acknowledgements

Many years of experience have gone into the writing of this book. I thank God for the Holy Spirit, who has truly been my teacher, friend, helper, and guide. He has taught me invaluable lessons on prayer, from the 3- to 4-year-old little girl in Missouri, to the wife, mother, and grandmother that I am today. To Linda Lee and Saundra, your feedback and editorial input gave me hope and direction during a time of great need. To Pat, Brenda, Debbie, and Johnetta: the seed for "The Womb of Your Prayers" was conceived in the 90s when we were being trained for ministry and has gestated in my spiritual womb over the years. I believe we have found our voices and places as women in ministry. May you continue to persevere and grow in the gospel, and the call of God upon your lives.

Chapter 1

THE WOMB OF YOUR PRAYERS

"My little children, of whom I travail in birth [prayer] *again until Christ be formed in you."*
(Galatians 4:19)

Monica was only twelve years old when it happened. A man, the uncle of one of her middle school friends, abducted her from home at knife point.

It was late at night and she was home alone. "I'll be right back," her mother had said, as she left to go to the store. She had left Monica at home by herself many times before and thought nothing of it as she jumped into her car and drove off.

There was a knock at the door shortly after. No one was home to help her. Monica thought she was safe, however, when she looked through the peep hole and saw the familiar face of her classmate's uncle. She was sadly mistaken.

What happened to Monica over the next few hours would be forever branded in her mind. But what sustained her, then and even now, is that she could *feel* the strength of her grandmother's prayers.

"Everything is going to be alright," she told herself. "I'm not by myself. Gramma's prayers are with me and they're going to get me out of this."

Those prayers acted as a blanket of protection and gave Monica hope throughout her ordeal. They were her focal point and the driving force that gave her the courage to escape what could have ended in tragedy.

The Power of Prayer

There is power in prayer. Just as Monica could *feel* her grandmother's prayers and was empowered by them, the words that come out of your mouth when you pray act as a blanket to cover and sustain those for whom you pray.

Have you ever told someone that you have been praying for them? Some people will simply say thanks, while others will thank you and say they "felt" your prayers. In other words, the power of God released as you interceded for them could be tangibly felt, and it undergirded and strengthened them.

Prayer can be likened to an invisible floor. You cannot see it, yet you step onto it by faith, much like Peter did when Jesus bid him to come and he walked on water at Christ's command (see Matthew 14:28).

Although prayer is invisible to your natural eyes, it is a supernatural force undergirded by the Holy Spirit, acting as an incubator in your spiritual womb and waiting for you to push out the thing for which you pray.

A Secure Sanctuary

The womb is a secure sanctuary for both human life and prayer. God created the womb of a woman to act as an incubator—an enclosed place in which embryos are kept in a controlled environment for protection and care until they are brought forth into the earth.

There is neither male nor female in the kingdom of God. Men as well as women have *spiritual* wombs. This is where the prayers you pray are housed. Your prayers are released as seed, which is fertilized by the words you speak and are incubated in your spiritual womb.

Just as a baby grows in his or her mother's womb in the natural, so does the seed of your prayers grow in your spiritual womb. Unlike the predictable timeline of the natural gestation process, no one but God can determine when the person, place, or thing for which you are praying will be born, or made manifest, in the earth.

Spiritual Gestation

The word *gestate* means "to carry a fetus in the womb from conception to birth." The normal gestation period for women is forty weeks. It varies for animals. For example, the gestation period for an elephant is approximately two years. It takes fourteen to sixteen months for a giraffe to give birth. Can you imagine?

The great patriarch, Abraham, was pregnant for twenty-five years with the promise that God had given him of a son (see Genesis 12-22). The answer to Abraham's prayer— Isaac—was conceived the *first time* he prayed. Yet, he carried the answer God had promised him in his spiritual womb until the time of delivery, which was two-and-a-half decades later. This is called a spiritual gestation period.

Stages of Development

The beautiful thing about the miracle of life is that information is available for you to follow the development of the baby growing inside of your natural womb, so you know what it looks like at various stages of growth. Each stage is chronicled, from the detection of the baby's heartbeat at approximately ten to twelve days, to the formation of its eyes, limbs, movements, etc.

Although such information regarding the developmental stages of the prayer seed growing inside of you does not exist in the natural, you can rest assured that as you pray, a similar development is occurring inside of your spiritual womb, even if you cannot see it with your naked eye. The key to giving birth to spiritual seed is staying the course and never—ever—walking away from your prayer assignment. Whether you can see it or not, the seed of God's Word is alive and active, and is always coming into a place of maturation and, ultimately, birth.

Chapter 2

STAYING POWER

"Let us not be weary in well doing for in due season we shall reap, if we faint not."
(Galatians 6:9)

You are instrumental in bringing your prayers to pass. As noted in Chapter 1, God answers your prayers the first time you pray, but you must watch over your spiritual seed to bring it to full maturation. Just as a hen sits on her eggs until they hatch, you must "brood" over your prayers.

The Holy Spirit "brooded" over the face of the waters in Genesis 1 as God created the heavens and the earth. As an intercessor, you should brood over the seed in your spiritual womb and place a protective cover over it. One of the ways this is done is by praying the Word over what you are asking God for and allowing it to incubate inside of your spirit.

First John 5:14-15 guarantees an answer to prayer when you base it upon scripture.

> *"And this is the confidence that we have in him, that, if we ask any thing according to his **will**, he heareth us. And if we know that he hears us, whatsoever we ask, we know that we have the petitions that we desired of him."*

God's Word is His will. Find scriptures to support your requests and pray these verses as you intercede. For example, if you are praying for someone who is stricken with fear, search your concordance for scriptures on fear, such as II Timothy 1:7. Personalize the scripture by praying, "Father, I thank You that You've not given (insert the person's name) a spirit of fear, but of power, and of love, and of a sound mind." In addition to praying for that person, declare this scripture over them until God directs you to pray something else or for someone else.

The same principle applies to any area of need—health and healing, finances, children, etc. Brood over your prayers by praying the Word. This will build a fortress around your spiritual seed. It will also increase your faith so you will be less likely to terminate your prayer assignment and abort what is growing inside of you.

As a pastor's wife, I have seen countless people walk away from their harvest after years and years of painstaking tenacity and intercession. Because of discouragement, strife, and/or other works of the flesh, they threw in the towel and deserted their harvest just when it was time to put in the sickle.

Can you imagine carrying your child (or if you are a man, your wife carrying your child) to term only to decide, just as the baby's head is in position to come forth and the water breaks, that you are not going to go through with it? No matter how ridiculous this sounds, this is what happens in the spirit too many times to men and women of God who abort their prayer assignments.

No Fainting Allowed

Rizpah is one of my favorite female Bible characters. Her story demonstrates steadfastness and perseverance, both attributes that are necessary for answered prayer. She was one of King Saul's concubines and had two sons by him. Because of Saul's sins against the Gibeonites, her sons were hanged on the gallows along with five sons that Saul had by other concubines.

Distraught, she demanded a proper burial for her children. Second Samuel 21:10 says Rizpah *"took sackcloth, and spread it upon the rock, from the beginning of harvest until water dropped upon* (her sons) *out of heaven, and suffered neither the birds of the air to rest on* [their dead, decaying bodies] *by day, nor the beasts of the field by night."*

Rizpah brooded over her sons. They were put to death at the beginning of harvest season. Verse 10 says she persevered in her efforts until it rained from heaven, which would have been approximately three months later at the end of the season. Can you imagine living out in the elements for three months, watching the bodies of your children decay as you fight off the birds of the air by day and the beasts of the field by night?

Although her behavior was probably viewed as extreme, her diligence paid off. King David heard about Rizpah and intervened. He gave her two sons, the other five boys who were hanged, AND Saul and his son Jonathan a proper burial. Because of Rizpah's prayers and intercession, her children *and* seven additional people benefitted from her three-month-long vigil. Who is benefitting from your steadfast prayers and intercession?

First Thessalonians 5:17 says to "pray without ceasing." This means that regardless of the gestation period, you should take a position before God and stand until you sense in your spirit that the Lord has heard and answered your prayers.

Travailing in Prayer, Again

The Apostle Paul said he would travail in prayer for the Galatians until Christ be formed in them *again*, which indicates Christ *had been* formed in them through intercession. However, they either backslid or became lukewarm toward God, so Paul had to begin travailing in prayer all over again.

The use of the word "travail" refers to the painful, laborious process of giving birth. Ask any woman and she will tell you that labor and delivery bring some of the worst pain a woman can ever experience. As an intercessor, you should expect to labor in your prayer closet until the seed on the inside of your spiritual womb comes to full maturity and manifestation. It will be painful at times, especially when you see signs of breakthrough and then defeat as the person you are praying for resumes their old behavior.

Expect to fight. You may have to ward off prayer robbers, such as doubt and unbelief, spirits of fear, discouragement, and rebellion, which could even come *from* the people for whom you pray. Answered prayer is a process. It will not happen overnight, so be like Rizpah—persevere and do not give up.

You will never know until you get to heaven the difference your prayers have made. One thing is certain, however: prayer is powerful, and God desires to express this power through you as His mouthpiece on the earth.

Chapter 3

CONDUITS OF PRAYER

"Cry aloud, spare not, lift up thy voice like a trumpet."
(Isaiah 58:1)

God created you as a mouthpiece—a speaking spirit, just a little lower than the angels (see Psalm 8:5). As such, He expects you to have a big mouth for Him; that is, to be a conduit of prayer. A "conduit" is a channel or pipe for conveying water or fluids. It is also a tube or duct for enclosing electric wires or cables.

Through prayer, you act as a "channel" through which God establishes His will on the earth while stopping the destructive plans of the enemy. You also operate as a "duct" in which He can enclose His Holy Spirit so that you can express His voice on the earth as you discern what is on the Lord's heart in any given moment.

The Heart of God

You would probably draw a blank stare if you asked the average Christian what is on the *heart* of God. But out of everything ever written on this subject, this is one of the purest purposes for intercession—to find out what is on the Father's heart and to express it as a conduit through prayer.

While most Christians have learned to pray "me-centered" prayers that focus on what they want or what they need—even if they are praying for someone else—the more mature intercessors have learned to listen for the Father's heart during their quiet times with Him, and to yield their voices as trumpets to the nations. These people have learned the real meaning of "intimacy" with God and experience it as they pray.

Are You a Martha or a Mary?

Martha was a workaholic and Mary was a student of the Bible. Martha was too busy working to spend time with the Lord, who was in her house teaching. Mary, on the other hand, sat at Jesus's feet, holding onto His every word.

In Luke 10:40, Martha accused Mary of being lazy and asked Jesus to make her get up and help her serve. Jesus refused her request. He told Martha that she was overwhelmed with much busyness and worry. Her sister Mary, on the other hand, had chosen "the good part" by being a student hearer of that which was said.

Martha had lost sight of what was important. As intercessors, it is easy to lose sight of your priorities and become overwhelmed by the affairs of this life. If you are not careful, days and weeks will pass before you realize that you have slacked off on your prayer assignment or have abandoned your prayer perch altogether.

This would be tragic with a natural pregnancy, as the baby in your womb depends on you for daily nourishment. It would be just as tragic spiritually; that is why it is important to sit continually at the Master's feet in fellowship and prayer.

He Wants to Commune with You

God desires your fellowship. He is grieved when you are too busy to spend time with Him in prayer. I knew a lady years ago who lived in a studio apartment and was going through a difficult period in her life. Because her place was so small, or perhaps because it was the closest thing to an altar in her apartment, she made the area in front of her kitchen sink her place of prayer. So, every day for months, she would meet God at a specific time and kneel in front of that sink to pray.

One day she went into the kitchen to pour herself a glass of water when, lo and behold, the presence of God manifested. The lady said He was so happy to see her. She said she laughed and told the Lord, "I was just coming to get a glass of water, but come on, we can fellowship."

Now, you and I both know that God knew she was just coming to get a glass of water. However, I believe He wanted to demonstrate to this woman how much He cherished their times together. Not only was He happy to see her, but she sensed His presence and His heart in that moment—He desired to spend some time with His daughter, which is what most parents would want to do if their child came into their presence.

Prayer is not an "exercise" that you do when you are in need. It may be birthed out of necessity, but after a period of time it becomes relational, as illustrated by this woman's story.

Chapter 4

ANOTHER COMFORTER

"And I will pray the Father, and he shall give you another Comforter, that he may abide with you forever." (John 14:16)

Contrary to popular belief, prayer is not reserved for the "prayer elites." If you are a Christian and call on the name of Jesus, God has anointed you to pray. Although you may feel inadequate and think that Sister Chief Intercessor or the Rev. So Righteous are more anointed to pray than you are, *Y-O-U* can pray. Why? Because the Bible says so!

First Thessalonians 5:17 admonishes all Christians to *"pray without ceasing,"* while Luke 18:1 says *"men* (and women, too) *ought always to pray and not to faint."* Prayer is "caught," not "taught." In other words, the more you pray, the more adept you will become at doing it and the more God's anointing and the mantle for prayer will rest upon you. You will develop a passion for prayer and make it a part of your everyday life.

One of the prerequisites for effective praying is training your spirit to become God-inside minded, i.e., cultivating your spirit to hear God's voice regardless of what you are doing. Some people call this "dual listening"—listening for God's still, small voice regardless of your busyness or the din of noise around you.

Practice developing an awareness of God and hearing the voice of the Holy Spirit. He is *always* speaking. Are you in a business or ministry meeting? Listen for God's voice. Are you in the middle of closing on a house? Listen for God's voice. Kids cutting up? Listen for God's voice. You get the picture.

I know people who are in constant communication with God. While most people who travel are focused on reaching their destinations or appreciating the beauty of the world around them, these people are praying and engaged in warfare, decreeing the Word of God over the atmosphere and over the animals, homes, and fields as they fly on an airplane or drive along the nation's highways.

These people are pregnant with prayer. You can find them in the middle of a social gathering praying in the Spirit and listening to God, while those around them are laughing and talking to one another. They pray as they turn over in their beds at night or wherever they go. No, they are not so heavenly minded that they are no earthly good, but they have developed a walk with God that is both intimate and habitual.

A Helping Hand

Unlike clothing labeled "one size fits all," one prayer does not fit all circumstances. God is not confined to a box, so you should learn how to pray outside of it. How? By the leading of the Holy Spirit.

The Holy Spirit was sent to the earth in Christ's stead. As Jesus prepared His disciples for His impending departure, they were sad because after three years of intense training and one-on-one ministry, they thought they were suddenly going to be left alone as orphans. Jesus, however, encouraged them not to be troubled, explaining that He would send them "another Comforter," which is the Holy Spirit, who would *abide with* (them) *forever*" (John 14:16).

Like Jesus, the Holy Spirit was sent to communicate directly from God to the disciples. He plays the same role in the lives of Christians today, which is why it is important for believers, especially those who are called to pray, to train their spirits to hear His voice—the voice of God in the earth.

Fumbling for Words

Do you remember what it was like when you first began to pray? You were probably nervous and afraid because you did not know what to say or how to pray. "What will the people in the prayer circle think of me as I fumble for words?" you may have asked yourself.

As you grow in your relationship with the Lord, however, you will discover that you are not the one who is praying. The Holy Spirit is the One who prayed (and still prays) through you. All you have to do is open your mouth and pray what you hear Him saying.

The Holy Spirit is an active voice and formidable force in prayer. He directs your times of prayer and intercession, because you, as a mere human, do not know what or how to pray. This is especially comforting since John 16:13 says the Holy Spirit—like Jesus did during His earthly ministry—sees, hears, and knows what is going on in the realm of the spirit.

It's Crowded in Here!

You are not alone when you pray. As soon as you open your mouth and assume the position, your prayer closet becomes crowded as you activate the angelic host and invite the godhead to become intimately involved in your times of intercession.

Because you do not know what prayer to offer, or how to offer it worthily, the Holy Spirit *meets* your "supplication"—the action of asking or begging for something earnestly or humbly—in the air, or by implication, in the realm of the spirit.

*"So too the [Holy] Spirit comes to our aid and bears us up in our weakness; for we do not know what prayer to offer nor how to offer it worthily as we ought, but the Spirit Himself **goes to meet** our supplication and pleads in our behalf with unspeakable yearnings and groanings too deep for utterance. And He Who searches the hearts of men knows what is in the mind of the [Holy] Spirit [what His intent is] because the Spirit intercedes and pleads [before God] in behalf of the saints according to and in harmony with God's will."* (Romans 8:26-27 AMP)

The Holy Spirit comes to your assistance and literally undergirds you in your human weakness and inability to pray. Remember, you are just the mouthpiece; He does all the work. He will teach you how to focus your prayers and how to pray strategically so you do not pray amiss. How? By praying through you.

As you daily commune with the Lord in your garden of prayer—or in front of your kitchen sink as referenced in the early part of this chapter—your prayer life will take on a whole new meaning. Instead of saying rote, lifeless prayers, the compassion and heart of God will begin flowing out of you by the power of the Holy Spirit and your prayer life will be elevated to another dimension.

Chapter 5

THE WORK OF THE SPIRIT

"So too the [Holy] Spirit comes to our aid...for we do not know what prayer to offer nor how to offer it worthily as we ought."
(Romans 8:26 AMP)

The Old Testament does not mention Jesus or the Holy Spirit by name. The Levitical priests, not Jesus, were the mediators between God and man. God spoke directly to the prophets, who were His mouthpiece, and the priests atoned for the sins of the children of Israel. This was done by the continual sacrificing of sheep, lambs, and other animals as mandated by the Law to cleanse Israel before a holy God.

This Old Testament picture is a foreshadowing of Jesus Christ, the New Testament High Priest who atoned for man's sins at the cross by shedding His blood on Calvary once and for all. It is also a foreshadowing of the Holy Spirit, who aids today's believers in prayer.

Romans 8:26 points to an Old Testament type and shadow for prayer. It says, *"So too the [Holy Spirit] comes to our aid. For we do not know what prayer to **offer** nor how to **offer** it worthily"* (AMP).

This scripture likens prayer to the Old Testament sacrifices where specific animals were offered up and sacrificed to God in certain ways and at certain times. Please note that not only were the types of sacrifices important in the Old Testament, but the *way* in which they were offered up to God was a matter of life and death.

If the Levitical priests, who were responsible for offering animal sacrifices to atone for the people's sins, did not follow God's instructions to the letter as stated in the Law, and deviated in any way, they not only lost their lives but their animal sacrifices were not accepted and the sins of the people for whom they were interceding went unforgiven.

Can you imagine what would happen if the prayers you offer up to God were rejected due to a technicality? What would then be the consequence of the people for whom you were praying?

Unspeakable Yearnings and Groanings

Thank God the New Testament church does not have a book of the Law that regulates what, when, or how to offer up prayers. No, the Holy Spirit runs interference for believers and acts as an umpire who has the spiritual rulebook and knows which prayers are necessary for each play.

He knows what prayers to offer, when to offer them, and how to offer them worthily. He does this by taking your prayers and praying through you with *"unspeakable yearnings and groanings"*—sounds—that cannot be articulated. This means that not only can your prayers be *felt*, as was the case with Monica and her grandmother in Chapter 1, but your prayers also have a *sound* that only the Holy Spirit can utter.

Not every prayer consists of words. Sometimes it is a sigh or a groan. I remember hearing a testimony on Christian television of a woman who had died and gone to heaven. She was standing before the Father, talking to Him. Although I do not recall the details of their conversation, she said she looked back to see her earthly father standing beside her lifeless body in the hospital bed. Suddenly he sighed, and immediately she went back into her body.

Although her father did not utter a word, the "unspeakable yearnings and groanings" of his sigh were sufficient enough to cause her to return into her body. The Holy Spirit prayed *the perfect will of God* through the release of her father's sigh, and the woman's life was extended.

What was the language of the sound of the sigh? Only God knows, but if her father was like any other parent, his sigh acted as a prayer that said, "Oh, God! Please don't take my daughter! Please, God! Not now!"

The "perfect will of God" prayed by the Holy Spirit, as referenced in Romans 8:26, can be interpreted as what was best for this lady in God's eternal plan of salvation for her life. It could not be articulated in the human language.

Holy Boldness

God's Word is His will—His last will and testament to believers. First John 5:14-15 says that you can have confidence the Father has heard and answered your prayers when you pray according to His will by the leading of the Holy Spirit.

Another word for "confidence" is *boldness*. Hebrews 4:16 says, *"Let us therefore come boldly unto the throne of grace, that we may obtain mercy, and find grace to help in time of need."*

Some believers lack confidence in their ability to pray. They do not believe they are worthy enough to approach God in prayer. Surely, they say, He will not hear or answer me. Others see themselves as grasshoppers. Still others lack confidence in their ability to intercede for others, much like Moses did when he questioned his ability to speak to Pharaoh on God's behalf.

This is where the Holy Spirit comes in. As you yield to Him, the sacrifice of prayers that you offer up will be received as a sweet-smelling aroma to God, and your prayer life will be transformed from a place of mediocrity and/or timidity, to a place of boldness, triumph, and power.

Chapter 6

LORD, TEACH US TO PRAY

"After this manner therefore pray ye:
Our Father which art in heaven."
(Matthew 6:9)

All God wants is a yielded vessel. You would be amazed at the people He uses in prayer. You will find that some of the meekest, most common and unassuming people are the most powerful in the prayer arena.

God uses ordinary people like you and me through the simple act of prayer. I can remember praying as a three- or four-year-old little girl who believed in the big God way up in the dark, starry sky. I remember always feeling insecure and afraid, which caused me to pray for my entire family every night as I went to bed.

While the Lord's prayer serves as a model prayer for some people today who may not know how to pray, I used the "Now I lay me down to sleep, I pray the Lord my soul to keep" prayer model when I was a child. Although I was not reared in a Christian home, I learned when I went to Sunday school to pray to God for the protection and peace I so desired. He heard and answered my prayers.

Prevailing in Prayer

According to James 5:16, the prayers of the righteous avail much. The word *avail* means, "the effective use in the achievement of a specific goal or objective." The Bible is replete with examples of men and women who have prayed effectively to achieve their goals and/or objectives—the answers to their prayers.

Some biblical examples of people who changed the course of history through prayer include:

➤ **Abraham,** the "father of faith," who interceded for the cities of Sodom and Gomorrah when God threatened to destroy them from the face of the earth (see Genesis 18:16-33).

➤ **Moses,** who knew God "face to face" and interceded for the Israelites on numerous occasions when God threatened to destroy them (see Exodus 32:7-14).

➤ **David,** a man "after God's own heart," who cried out to God in prayer, praise, and worship in times of peace as well as in times of trouble (see Psalms 34, 35 and 103).

➤ **Hannah,** who, tired of being vexed in her soul because she was barren, cried out to God in her anguish, pleading for a male child until God heard and answered her prayer (see I Samuel 1:1-28).

➤ **Anna,** a New Testament prophetess of "great age" who devoted her life to serving God in the temple—fasting and praying night and day—saw the Lord's Christ when He was taken to the temple to be dedicated (see Luke 2:36-38).

➤ **Jesus,** God in the flesh, who interceded for mankind as He prepared to go to the cross and is yet making intercession for you before the Father in heaven (see John 17:9-20; Hebrews 7:25).

You can probably think of people in your own life or sphere of influence who prevail in prayer—or, as they say, people who "can get a prayer through." The important thing to remember is that God, unlike man, does not have favorites. He is looking for yielded vessels that will surrender to the gentle leading of the Holy Spirit and do not mind being poured out as a drink offering through prayer. He can use one person or a multitude. Can He count on you?

Chapter 7

THE POWER OF ONE

*"And the men turned their faces from thence, and went toward
Sodom: but Abraham stood yet before the LORD. And
Abraham drew near, and said...."* **(Genesis 18:23a)**

It was a dark day in the history of the United States in
June 1962, when the Supreme Court ruled that the
state-mandated recitation of prayer by every student, vol-
untarily or not, was unconstitutional (Engel v. Vitale). This
was the beginning of a satanic movement across the U.S. to
remove God, and ultimately the very acknowledgement of
His Son Jesus and Christian symbols, from public society
and all levels of government.

From that day forward, not only was state mandated
praying in public schools ruled unconstitutional, but
praying in the name of Jesus has also been gradually elim-
inated in many federal and state proceedings.

Although America was founded by men who believed in *the* sovereign God and prayer, the devil has succeeded over the years in using atheists, agnostics, intellectuals, liberals, marginal Christians, and the like to eradicate God from every aspect of public and private life.

Consequently, there are *generations* of people who do not know the God of Abraham, Isaac or Jacob—the God of the Bible—because He has been removed from a place of preeminence and can only be taught at home and/or at church. They do not realize He wants to have a relationship with them.

A Crisis of Prayerlessness

Over the years, the American church has become the "prayer-less church." *Surely you jest*, you might say, but take a look at how many people show up for intercessory prayer at any given church on any given night, or on Sunday mornings for pre-service prayer. The last time I checked, the saints were not running over top of each other trying to get into the sanctuary to pray.

Granted, there are pockets of people praying in the United States and across the world, especially since the onset of the coronavirus pandemic. As a whole, however, the U.S. Body of Christ is experiencing a crisis of prayerlessness—in the church and at home. As such, people use prayer as a last resort and the Body of Christ appears to be spiritually anemic.

Unlike Enoch, who walked in habitual fellowship with God, the 21ˢᵗ Century church seems to have lost its zeal for fellowship and intimacy with the Father. Prayer has become a casual exercise that born-again believers do as they drift off to sleep at night or leave home for work in the morning, or when they have a dire emergency.

There is no doubt that Jesus's question to His disciples whether they would tarry with Him in prayer for one hour, would be met with a resounding "No!" by today's body of believers (see Matthew 26:40). I am convinced, however, that the reason most Christians do not pray more often is not because they are lazy, but because they do not know how, nor do they understand, the value of prayer.

The average Christian has not been taught the ABCs of faith, much less the fundamentals of prayer, and therefore does not understand prayer's significance, or for what or how to pray. Consequently, most Christians do not have a passion for prayer or an understanding of its dynamics.

War Room

The amplified version of James 5:16 says prayer "*makes tremendous power available*" to those who pray. Just imagine: the simple act of prayer not only changes people and situations, but can release the power of God to change an entire nation.

Think about it, the power of one individual who prays can change the destiny of a nation, just as one individual's lawsuit was ultimately responsible for removing state-mandated prayer from the U.S. public school system forever.

The mother-in-law of the Rev. Dr. David Yonggi Cho, the South Korean pastor of one of the world's largest churches, is an example of what I refer to as "the power of one." She was pregnant with the salvation of her nation. She carved out a "war room" in the side of a mountain and reportedly drove out communism in South Korea and birthed Christianity into that nation through prayer.

In another instance, when South Korea was completely destitute after the Korean War, this same woman went to a mountain in Jori-myeon, Paju, to pray for God to send money to meet the needs of the ministry and to build their church—the Yoido Full Gospel Church.

Five hundred women joined her to fast and pray *for three months*. Not only did God send the money to build their church, but **one million souls were saved**— birthed—through prayer. God also protected South Korea from North Korean invasion because of their intercession. It only takes one, and the power of that one praying person is not to be underestimated.

Father Abraham

Abraham, the "father of faith," is a biblical example of one person who dared to pray to, and believe in, the God of the universe. He interceded for the cities of Sodom and

Gomorrah in Genesis 18:16-33, when God threatened to destroy them from the face of the earth.

Abraham's walk with God was so close that God hesitated to leave him after a divine visitation, and questioned whether He should share with Abraham what He was about to do:

> *"And the LORD said, Shall I hide from Abraham that thing which I do; Seeing that Abraham shall surely become a great and mighty nation, and all the nations of the earth shall be blessed in him? For,* **I know him***, that he will command his children and his household after him, and they shall keep the way of the LORD, to do justice and judgment; that the LORD may bring upon Abraham that which he hath spoken of him?"* (Genesis 18:17-19)

The word *know* in this context refers to "intimacy," the kind that husbands and wives experience during sexual intercourse as they become "one flesh." God was saying that Abraham had forged a relationship with Him through prayer and faith, and that God Himself was confident of Abraham's character and integrity to raise his children after God, and to keep the way of the Lord.

Because Abraham had become amalgamated—or joined together into a whole—with God, the Lord felt compelled to tell His "friend" His plans to destroy Sodom and Gomorrah. No doubt Abraham had been praying for his nephew Lot and his family who lived in these godless cities and would have been affected by their destruction, much like multitudes were affected by the bombing of the World Trade Center on that fateful day of September 11, 2001, and the coronavirus pandemic that devastated the world in 2020.

God is Faithful

> "And the men rose up from thence, and looked toward Sodom: and Abraham went with them to bring them on the way…And the LORD said, Because the cry of Sodom and Gomorrah is great, and because their sin is very grievous; I will go down now, and see whether they have done altogether according to the cry of it, which is come unto me; and if not, I will know. And the men turned their faces from thence, and went toward Sodom: but Abraham stood yet before the LORD. And Abraham drew near, and said…." (Genesis 18:16-23a)

The beautiful thing about the Lord is that He is willing to answer your prayers. As wise as a serpent but harmless as a dove, Abraham demonstrated humility and referential fear of God as he asked Him to spare Sodom and Gomorrah for ten righteous people (see Genesis 18:32).

God will honor your requests just as He did Abraham's, who started out by asking God to spare the city for fifty righteous people and worked his way down to ten. Unfortunately, there were fewer than ten righteous people in Sodom and Gomorrah. However, the important thing to remember is that God agreed to spare the cities for ten people who walked upright before Him.

I remember praying for a woman once who was about to undergo a delicate surgical procedure. We agreed in prayer and I asked God to enable her body to "open up" and respond to the operation that was going to take place. Well, the woman's doctor was surprised at how easily things went. She said the woman's body just "opened up," and she performed the surgery in no time flat and without complications.

The Lord will honor your prayer requests just as quickly as He will the intercession of a multitude. He is looking for that one individual who loves Him enough to walk in habitual fellowship with Him and to yield himself as a vessel of prayer. As you do this, the power of the Holy Spirit will rest upon you and you will find supernatural help in your prayer endeavors.

Chapter 8

ALL MANNER OF PRAYER

*"Pray at all times (on every occasion, in every season) in the
Spirit, with all [manner of] prayer and entreaty."*
(Ephesians 6:18a AMP)

There are many types of prayers. Although the following
list is not exhaustive, it will give you an example of the
types of prayers, or prayer models, that can be used in your
own times of communing with the Lord. As you become
more adept at praying, your reliance upon the Holy Spirit
to pray through you will become more natural, and He will
begin to flow through you like rivers of living water.

Praise & Thanksgiving

This type of prayer focuses on praising and thanking
God for His blessings (see Psalm 150). When I first learned
how to pray, I thought prayer consisted of bringing a list

of requests before the Lord and enumerating them one-by-one. But guess what? Once the list ended, so did my time of prayer.

While there is nothing seemingly wrong with presenting the Lord with a "honey-do" list, sometimes He just wants you to thank and praise Him for His goodness and His blessings. Like most parents, God delights in blessing His children who adore Him and do not have an agenda when they come into His presence.

There is nothing more irritating than when the only time you hear from your children or certain people is when they have a crisis and/or need advice or financial assistance. Is this the kind of relationship you have with your heavenly Father? I hope not. Plus, the prayer of praise and thanksgiving is more for you than it is for God.

The more you thank and praise Him, the better you will feel and the more your circumstances will begin to line up with what you are praying. The more your circumstances begin to line up, the more they will begin to reflect God's goodness and greatness in your life.

Corporate Prayer

The enemy would love nothing better than to isolate you from the Body of Christ, especially in prayer. My husband and I had the pleasure of visiting Israel with a group of pastors and intercessors from throughout the United States. We were warned during our stay to never go anywhere alone, even if you were a man, because tourists were easy prey for predators.

Even parents in the United States warn their children to walk with other children because it is easier to fight off an attack when a child is in a crowd than it is when he or she is alone. Corporate prayer operates in a similar capacity. When you assemble to pray with other believers, your prayer power is multiplied exponentially and enables you to do spiritual warfare on a larger scale than when you pray alone.

Truly, one prayer warrior (like Dr. Cho's mother-in-law) can put a thousand demonic forces to flight, but the Bible says two will cause 10,000 demonic spirits to flee. *Five hundred* women joined Dr. Cho's mother-in-law in prayer. Can you imagine the spiritual pressure applied to the spirit realm as these women cried out for souls and their nation?

The intensity of the prayer assault increases as the number of people multiplies, *and* the chances of spiritual backlash will be lessened because of the corporate anointing (see Leviticus 26:8; Deuteronomy 32:30; Acts 12:5; and Acts 16:25-26).

Prayer of Committal or Consecration

This is a prayer of surrender and/or consecration when a person relinquishes his desires to the plan of God and is set apart for a specific purpose. Jesus prayed this kind of prayer in Matthew 26:39 when He was in the Garden of Gethsemane.

He understood His purpose for coming to the earth was to die on the cross. He knew that His assignment was to deliver mankind from death, hell, and the grave. Still, Jesus cried out to God to remove "this cup"—the cross—from Him, because part of the dying process was taking on the sins of the world, which would separate Him from His heavenly Father for the first time in eternity.

Nevertheless, Jesus surrendered and said, *"Not my will, but thine be done."* Likewise, the more intimate you become in prayer with God, the more apparent His plan and purpose for your life will become. Once this happens, you will find yourself more than willing to relinquish what you desire and say "yes" to what He wants for you. After a while, you will discover that His will for your life is far greater than anything you could ever ask, think, or imagine.

Prayer of Petition

Luke 18:1-5 is about a widow who has been taken advantage of. She petitions a judge to right the wrong. We do not know the details surrounding her circumstances— perhaps a relative or someone is trying to take the property left as an inheritance to her by her late husband. What we do know, however, is that she is in legal trouble.

She petitions the judge until he agrees to do what she is asking. The scripture says the judge's heart was hardened toward her initially, but because she continued asking and would not give up, he eventually granted her request, lest she "weary" him in the process.

The prayer of petition is a prayer model that can be used when you are facing a challenging or desperate situation and the answer to your prayer is not forthcoming. Perhaps you are faced with a legal matter and are running out of resources and/or time, or you have been praying for years for a loved one who seems to be getting worse instead of better.

Simply put, you not only present a prayer request or grievance before the Father like the widow did to the unjust judge, but you repeatedly petition Him in prayer until you receive the answer you desire.

Now, I know some members of the Body of Christ teach that to ask God for something more than once is a sign of doubt and unbelief, but I beg to differ. The prayer of petition can be used when the Holy Spirit gives you a scripture to stand on, such as Isaiah 53:4-5, and you bring God into remembrance of what He said as you stand in faith for the healing of that person.

This type of prayer is not to be confused with presenting a "list" of prayer requests. The prayer of petition is very specific and urgent. Luke 18:1 says, "*Men ought always to pray, and **not to faint**.*" The implication here is that the weightiness of the matter the woman was dealing with could have overwhelmed her and caused her to give up hope. Instead, she began a petitioning process much like that of the U.S. court system until her grievance was finally heard and her request granted.

Like the widow in Luke 18, you may have to pray using the Word of God as your weapon until you receive the answer to your prayers. Jeremiah 23:29 says, *"Is not my word like as a fire? saith the Lord, and like a **hammer that breaketh the rock in pieces?"***

The word of God, when spoken by born again believers, consumes everything in its path. Nothing can withstand its power. And the anointing that rests upon your words will destroy every yoke and remove every mountain, boulder, or rock that stands between you and the answer to your prayers.

Prayer of Agreement

"Can two people walk together except they be agreed?" (Amos 3:3) The prayer of agreement is based on multiplied prayer power when two or more people come into agreement regarding the outcome of a situation (see Matthew 18:19).

This is different from corporate prayer in that the people do not necessarily have to assemble themselves together for prayer; they simply agree on a thing and pray accordingly in their individual prayer closets and at their convenience.

The important thing to note is that they agree on a plan of action and what they are going to ask for in prayer. It is also important to confirm that everyone is on the same page. If one person is praying contrary to what the other people are praying, it could cause confusion and delay the answer to that prayer or derail it altogether.

I remember listening to a husband and wife talk about this type of prayer. The husband had assumed his wife agreed with him as he took her hand and began praying for a new car, which would have put them deeper in debt. However, she interrupted him and told him she was not in agreement with him. Fortunately, he listened to her and they avoided over-extending themselves financially.

Although they were laughing when they shared this story with me, it was not a laughing matter when it first occurred. Assume nothing. Make sure you and your prayer partners—especially your spouse—agree on the specifics of your prayer.

Prayer of Binding and Loosing

Intercessors have a unique place in the Body of Christ. They operate as gatekeepers and watchmen on the wall. As watchmen, they peer into the distance to see what is brewing on the horizon so they can forewarn the prayer warriors and alert them on how and for what to pray.

As gatekeepers, they guard the city's spiritual gates. They determine who or what can or cannot enter their territory, as well as the kinds of activities that can or cannot take place within their city walls or the territory that they cover.

The prayer of binding and loosing operates in much the same manner. As an intercessor, you determine through prayer what activities take place in the lives of the people, places or things for which you pray. Do you see storm clouds on the horizon? Is there a certain activity taking place in your family, church, or national or state government? Through prayer, you determine what is or is not permissible, and heaven will back you up.

Matthew 18:18 says whatever you bind (or disallow) on earth will be bound (or disallowed) in heaven, and whatever you loose (or allow) on earth will be loosed (or allowed) in heaven.

This prayer model consists of more than just saying, "I bind you, Satan, and I loose the will of God in this situation." Be specific. Ask God for His will concerning the matter and listen for His answer. Perhaps He will lead you to scriptures, such as Psalm 91:10, which you can decree over the situation as you pray.

I remember praying with a group of people about an upcoming gubernatorial election. We were adamantly opposed to a certain person being elected and were praying in that regard. Suddenly, I saw the face of the opposing candidate and I knew God wanted me to pray for her. I told the group that I needed to pray for this person, although she was not our person of choice.

As I began to pray for this woman, the Lord showed me what He wanted to allow (or be loosed in) her life. I knew by the way the Holy Spirit was praying through me that God's will was for her to be elected. I heard myself asking God to soften her hardened heart and to heal her of the hurt and trauma she had experienced as a female politician in a man's world. I cried out for her salvation.

Although I never used the words "bind" or "loose," that is exactly what I was doing: agreeing with the will of God, and disagreeing with the will of man (and the devil) in the earth and our state government.

The prayer of binding and loosing is strategic because the Word guarantees that when you pray according to the leading of the Holy Spirit, heaven and the angelic hosts come to your aid to bring your words to pass. So, you can strategically target specific areas, such as the building of a racetrack in your community, or a gentleman's club, as you partner with God regarding what He wills to happen in society.

Remember, the purpose of prayer is to birth the will of God into the earth and to stop the schemes of the devil. Get into agreement with one another and the Holy Spirit and see how quickly God shifts what will, or will not take place, all because of your prayers.

Prayer of Intercession

The prayer of intercession is the act of mediating—of entering another person's spiritual battles through prayer. Because it is so complex and involved, it has been given its own section in the next chapter.

Chapter 9

Prayer of Intercession

"And he saw that there was no man, and wondered that there was no intercessor: therefore his arm brought salvation unto him, and his righteousness, it sustained him." (Isaiah 59:16)

Intercessors act as mediators—they enter another person's spiritual battles through prayer. Jesus did this on Calvary when He took on the sins (and sicknesses) of mankind.

I remember going to church years ago, and as I entered the sanctuary, a woman who was known for being a keen intercessor and prayer warrior, approached me and put my hand on her forehead. "Please pray for me!" she said.

As I opened my mouth to pray, I entered into overwhelming confusion and could barely utter a word. Suddenly, by the leading of the Holy Spirit, I broke forth into tongues and prayed in the Spirit until my natural tongue was released to intercede for her.

She shared with me afterwards that she had been battling confusion and insanity. Unbeknownst to me, when I began interceding for her as a mediator, I literally took on the confusion and mental state she was experiencing.

The Mediator

The word *mediate* means to settle disputes, such as a strike between employees and their employer; to reconcile. Hence, a mediator is one who acts on the behalf of another in their defense and tries to bring reconciliation, or an otherwise favorable outcome, to the situation or circumstance at hand. Attorneys do this when they intercede for their clients. Just as Jesus interceded, or mediated, for mankind on the cross, I mediated for this dear lady. I entered into the darkness and confusion that was trying to overtake her as I prayed that she would have peace and soundness of mind. You, too, act as a mediator—an intercessor—each time you pray.

Let's Get Physical

Intercession is by far the most physical of the various types of prayers written about in this book. By mere definition of the word, *intercession*—also known as spiritual warfare—means to collide, strike, or dash. The inference here is that this type of prayer involves a violent collision, much like two cars in an auto accident, or a confrontation of opposing spiritual forces, such as good and evil, light and darkness.

To intercede can also mean to encroach on or against— to intrude gradually and insidiously upon the domain, possessions, or rights of another, to trespass. If you were a hunter and you wanted to hunt on a property where a "NO TRESPASSING" sign was posted, you would have to get the property owner's permission. While this is true in the natural, thank God it does not work that way in the spirit. You do not need Satan's permission to encroach on his property, nor do you have to be apologetic.

Christ's death on Calvary has given you the legal right to intercede for mankind and to take back what the devil has stolen. In so doing, you have been delegated authority to do God's bidding in the earth. According to Luke 10:19, God has given you *"power to tread on serpents and scorpions, and over all the power of the enemy: and nothing shall by any means hurt you."* Not even the devil.

Be Violent

Another definition of the word *intercession* means "to push against by accident or violently." Have you ever been praying what you thought was going to be a nice *little* prayer and you "happened" upon a major battle? I was visiting a lady in the hospital once who was battling a terminal diagnosis. I was getting ready to leave and thought I would pray a nice "blessing" over her before I departed.

As I leaned down to pray, a demon manifested in her and stared me in the face. Her facial features became distorted and the demonic spirit threw her body across the bed. I was shocked!

I did not know what to do, but then I heard certain scriptures in my spirit and I began repeating them, using them like the hammer referred to in Jeremiah 23:29. After a while, the spirit was cast out of the woman and she was set free from demonic oppression.

What began as a simple act of prayer caused me to accidently stumble upon a spiritual stronghold in this woman, which became a violent overthrow of demonic rule in her life. The disease was meant to kill this dear lady, but because of intercession and the help of the Holy Spirit, the plans of the enemy were thwarted and the demonic forces had to obey the Word of God. Her issue was cursed at the root and literally withered and died, much like the fig tree Jesus cursed at the root in Mark 11:14.

Matthew 11:12 says, *"The kingdom of heaven suffereth violence, and the violent take it by force."* You will know the kingdom of heaven has come when you see the advancement of God's kingdom through miracles, signs, and wonders—when souls are saved, the deaf hear, the lame walk, and the oppressed are set free. This is a sign of the "violent" taking back God's territory by force and demonic rule being overthrown... through intercession.

Gap Standers, Hedge Builders

Have you ever purchased a new car and needed to take out "GAP insurance"? **G**uaranteed **A**sset **P**rotection protects you if your car is totaled by paying the remaining difference between the actual cash value of your vehicle and the balance stilled owed on the financing.

God has a similar plan for His creation called "standing in the gap." As a mediator between God and man, Jesus paid the difference between your actual value to God, who gave His only begotten Son, and the balance you owed because of your sins, which you could never pay in a million years.

Restorers of the Breach

Ezekiel 22:30 says, *"And I sought for a man among them, that should make up the **hedge**, and **stand** in the **gap** before me for the land, that I should not destroy it: but I found none."*

A great gulf exists between God and unregenerate man, which is why Jesus was sent to the earth *"to break down the middle wall of partition between us"* (Ephesians 2:14). Intercessors have a twofold responsibility in repairing this gap. First, to repair a wall or hedge that has been torn down, which suggests your prayers restore a breach in the wall caused by the devil and his cohorts (see Isaiah 58:12); and secondly, to stand in the gap and protect that wall against further infiltration by the enemy throughout the rebuilding process (see Nehemiah 6:1, 3).

In the natural, a "gap" is a break in the protective thorny hedge or wall of stones that surround a person, place or thing. Spiritually, gaps are formed and hedges are breached through personal sins, as well as family and national iniquities that are passed down from one generation to another. These iniquities may include alcoholism, terminal illnesses, perversion, premature deaths, idolatry, legalized abortions, or broken marriages.

When iniquitous sin begins to erode the fiber of a family or society, it leaves openings or gaps for enemy forces to invade and plunder. The break invites trouble. To bar intruders, someone has to stand guard until the gap can be repaired. You are that guard, through intercession.

When my husband and I were in Israel, I remember seeing cactus plants along the road that were covered with thorns. These were no ordinary thorns; they were several inches long and very thick. They covered the cacti like a protective barrier, making it all but impossible for animals or humans to get to the plants without sustaining severe bodily injury.

The cacti were "hedged in" by the thorns, which is what intercessors do—they form a protective wall around those for whom they pray, making it nearly impossible for the enemy to penetrate it. This is similar to the "brooding" mentioned in Chapter 2. As you hedge in that for which you pray through intercession, you are literally brooding over or covering the spiritual seed that is incubating in your spiritual womb. This is what is known as spiritual warfare.

Chapter 10

SPIRITUAL WARFARE

"For we wrestle not against flesh and blood, but against principalities, against powers, against the rulers of the darkness of this world, against spiritual wickedness in high places."
(Ephesians 6:12)

What is spiritual warfare? Simply put, it is opposition that comes against you in the spirit realm. The opposition is sometimes an unexpected attack, such as the assault on the World Trade Center in September 2001, or it is retaliatory in nature—like when the United States declared war on Iraq, Osama Bin Laden, and other terrorists in response to the September 11 attacks.

Although these are natural examples, spiritual warfare is not in the realm of the natural. It takes place in the realm of the supernatural—in the realm of the spirit—and can only be fought and won in the spirit with spiritual weapons that cannot be seen.

The Spirit Realm

The spirit realm is very real, more real than your five physical senses. Most Christians are more "sense" minded than "spirit" minded. They are led by what they see, hear, smell, touch, and taste, and are oblivious to what is going on in the spirit world around them.

As a matter of fact, some Christians do not believe that a spirit world exists. They limit the supernatural to the pages of the Bible or to old television series, such as *Bewitched* or the cartoon *Casper the Friendly Ghost*. However, the spirit realm does exist, and it is more real than the reflection of your face in the mirror.

I did not have to be convinced that a world existed outside of what I could see. I have had many encounters with spirits throughout my life, beginning when I was a young child. I remember being up late at night rummaging for food in the kitchen while the rest of the household was fast asleep, when "something" would touch me or call my name. This happened on more than one occasion, and needless to say, I would quickly forget about eating.

I can also remember, as I grew older, waking up in the night and seeing a man or a woman standing in the room looking at me—not to mention the times I have seen fleeting dark shadows out of the corner of my eye.

One encounter that stands out to me the most, however, occurred years ago when my son and I were visiting friends in another state. I was awakened out of my sleep one morning by loud banging noises coming from the kitchen. It sounded like someone was angrily slinging pots and throwing pans.

I went to the bedroom door and called my friend's name. The banging stopped. I knew in my spirit she was not there. (I found out later that she had gotten up early and taken her husband to work.) I did not say anything to anyone, however. Like Mary the mother of Jesus, I pondered what had happened in my heart.

My son, who was sleeping in another part of the house, later told me that he had seen shadows, one of which had crossed the room where he was sleeping and stood behind a tall plant. Although alarmed, I again held my peace, that is until I went into the kitchen later that day to fix myself something to eat. While in the kitchen, a voice called out to me: "*Sylvia.*"

I immediately rebuked the devil and told the couple in whose house we were staying. We began to pray over their home, anointing our kids and each room of the house with oil. Why am I sharing this with you? Because you need to *know* and be convinced that there is a world where angels and demons live and carry out the orders of their masters— be it God or the devil.

The Apostle Paul wrote in II Corinthians 2:11 that God does not want you to be ignorant of the devil's devices. One of the definitions for the word *device* is "a plan or scheme, especially to speak evil of, slander, or defame someone." The enemy's devices are the schemes and strategies that he plots in the spirit against you and the people, places, and things for which you pray.

Satan wants to use God's creation to make a mockery of Him, but do not take my word for it. The Bible says out of the mouth of two or three witnesses every word is established. Following are a few witnesses—biblical examples—that confirm the existence of the spirit realm, where destinies are fought for, lost, won, and/or stolen.

Hindering & Retaliatory Spirits

Have you ever wondered why it takes so long for your prayers to be answered? Or why, once you have broken through and received the answer to your prayers, all hell breaks loose against you? Or better yet, why hell seems to break loose *because* you are praying?

Many Christians want to blame God for the delay in answered prayer, but the answer for the delay is never on the sending end. It can be attributed to the warfare that takes place in the heavenlies from the time you utter the first prayer until the time that prayer is answered.

In Daniel 10, the prophet Daniel had fasted and prayed for twenty-one days for the understanding of one of the many visions God had shown him. God dispatched Gabriel, the messenger angel, to bring the answer to Daniel's prayer.

*"Then he said to me, Do not fear, Daniel, for **from the first day** that you set your heart to*

understand, and to humble yourself before your
God, your words were heard; and I have come
because of your words." (Daniel 10:12 Spirit-
Filled Life Bible)

The angel was dispatched to Daniel the first day—the very moment—he opened his mouth and prayed. However, he was delayed in the second heavens for twenty-one days by the demonic principality over the region of Persia, which is where Daniel resided.

But the prince of the kingdom of Persia withstood
me twenty-one days; and behold, Michael, one of
the chief princes, came to help me, for I had been
left alone there with the kings of Persia." (Daniel
10:13 Spirit-Filled Life Bible)

What you see in these two scriptures is a picture of the spiritual activity that takes place when you pray. To you, you are making a simple request to the Lord by the leading of His Spirit. "Lord," you might say, "please heal my neighbor and save his entire household." But to Satan, you are praying for God to overthrow his demonic rule and deliver the Smith family—your neighbors—from the generational curse of disease and premature death.

What seems like a simple request to you is huge by Satan's standards. Psalm 103:20 says the angels both *do* God's commandments and *hearken unto the voice of His word.* The word *hearken* means to hear intelligently, often with the implication of attention and obedience. You are the "voice" of God's word in the earth. Each time you pray or decree what thus saith the Lord, the angels hear and obey the words that you speak and are set in motion to answer your prayers.

Be forewarned, however, there are also spiritual entities waiting to bring to pass the words you speak that are contrary to God's word *and* your prayers. So, make your prayers count—only speak what you want to come to pass. Practice the ministry of silence instead of spewing forth venom and/or defeat when you become frustrated, angry, and/or discouraged.

You Are Not Exempt

Just as the angel told Daniel in verse 13 that the spiritual warfare was so fierce that Michael, the warring prince, had to come to his aid, angelic assistance is also dispatched to help you when you pray. Hence, Romans 8:26 should take on a whole new meaning; not only does the Holy Spirit come to your assistance when you pray, but so does God's angelic army.

"Wow!" you might say. "Just to bring the answer to one man's prayers?"

Yes, but please note that the warfare did not end when the answer was delivered to Daniel (nor will it end with the answer to your prayers). No; it continued as Gabriel prepared to go back to heaven.

He told Daniel in verse 20 that he would have twice the warfare returning to the throne room because the principalities of Persia *and* Greece were going to double team him. It is inferred that Gabriel would probably once again have to enlist the help of Michael. So, while he and Michael had to battle against *hindering* spirits to *bring* Daniel the answer to his prayers, they would have to war against *retaliatory* spirits as they *returned* to heaven.

Lying Spirit

In I Kings 22 (see also II Chronicles 18), we find an interesting story of two kings—Jehoshaphat, the king of Judah, and Ahab, the king of Israel. Ahab was an evil king and Jehoshaphat was a godly king who almost lost his life were it not for God's divine intervention.

If you know anything about Ahab, then you know he was married to Jezebel, one of the most wicked queens who has ever lived. Ahab and Jezebel had a co-dependent relationship. Ahab was lazy and relied on Jezebel to do his fighting for him. Jezebel did not mind because she was a domineering and controlling woman who loved power.

I am not sure where Jezebel was during this time, but we see Ahab propositioning King Jehoshaphat to go to war with him to win a piece of territory that he was too lazy or too afraid to try and possess by himself, although he had a great army of men fighting for him.

Evidently Jehoshaphat felt a little uneasy about the proposition, so he asked if there were any prophets who could seek God for direction as to whether he should involve himself in this military endeavor. Well, King Ahab had prophets galore—400, to be exact. They ALL lied to the king, promising him victory, saying, *"Go up, for the Lord will deliver it into the hand of the king"* (I Kings 22:6).

Still not completely certain whether he should align himself with Ahab, King Jehoshaphat asked if there was yet one more prophet. Ahab reluctantly called for Micaiah, whom he hated because, according to Ahab, Micaiah *"does not prophesy good concerning me, but evil"* (I Kings 22:8).

Ahab sent for Micaiah and an interesting thing occurred when he appeared. At first he mocked Ahab and agreed with the 400 lying prophets, but then he had a vision, which he shared with both kings, saying:

> *"I saw the Lord sitting on His throne, and all the host of heaven standing by, on His right hand and on the left. And the Lord said, 'Who will persuade Ahab to go up, that he may fall at Ramoth Gilead?' So one spoke in this manner, and another spoke in that manner. Then* **a spirit came forward** *and stood before the Lord and said, 'I will persuade him.' Then the Lord said to him, 'In what way?' So he said, 'I will go out and be a*

lying spirit in the mouth of all his prophets.' And the Lord said, 'You shall persuade him and also prevail. Go out and do so.'" (I Kings 22:19-22).

What you see here is a glimpse into the court of heaven—the realm of the spirit—where Ahab's destiny was decided, not because God was mad at him, but because he was one of the most wicked kings who had ever lived. God had given him opportunities to repent. Although he humbled himself before God in I Kings 21:29, he was still judged for his wickedness and rebellion. Therefore, the Lord allowed a *lying spirit* to persuade Ahab to go to war and he subsequently lost his life.

In John 8:44, Jesus called Satan "the father of lies," so it is not surprising that one of his minions appeared in the court of heaven and asked permission to destroy one of Satan's very own. Similar exchanges still take place today.

Pray and ask the Lord to open the eyes of your spiritual understanding so that you can hear what He hears and see what He sees. Understanding the spirit realm will aid you in understanding what is going on in the "real" world around you. It will also enable you to pray more accurately and effectively.

Accusing Spirit

Many people have heard the story of Job. He was a righteous man who loved God. Satan knew this and wanted to destroy him, just as he wants to destroy all of God's creation—especially the righteous. After years of studying Job, Satan was pretty certain he had found a "legal right" in which to accuse him, so he decided to pay God a visit.

> "Now there was a day when the sons (the angels)
> of God came to present themselves before the Lord,
> and Satan (the adversary and accuser) also came
> among them." (Job 1:6 AMP)

God addressed Satan and asked him where he had been. His response was that he had been *going to and fro on the earth and from walking up and down on it,*" (Job 1:7 AMP). Why? Because he was looking for some poor, unsuspecting soul he could accuse before God and ultimately destroy.

Satan has many names, one of which is the "accuser of the brethren." Just as the angels stand before God's throne and have access to the court of heaven, so do Satan and other demonic spirits, such as the lying spirit found in I Kings 22:21.

Satan probably began to accuse some of the individuals he had observed during his restless walk of going up and down and to and fro throughout the earth. Perhaps some of them were guilty and God could not render an innocent verdict on their behalf. But then God thought about His champion, Job.

"Have you considered my servant Job?" He asked. There *"is none like him on the earth, a blameless and upright man, one who [reverently] fears God and abstains from and shuns evil?"* (Job 1:8).

Satan, true to his character, began to accuse Job before God like a skilled attorney. He told the Father the only reason Job was serving Him was because God had placed a protective *hedge* around him, his family, and all his possessions (see Job 1:10).

"I'd serve you, too," he inferred, "but if you take all of these things from him, he will curse you to your face."

The hedge Satan refers to in verse 10 is the same one mentioned in Chapter 9. If you will recall, intercessors have a twofold responsibility: first, to repair a wall or *hedge* that has been torn down, which indicates your prayers restore a breach in the wall, and second, to stand in the gap and protect that wall against the enemy throughout the rebuilding process.

Satan asked God to remove the hedge of protection from around Job and all that pertained to him. God gave him permission to attack Job, but the Lord did not remove His hedge of protection—He just moved the boundaries out by a few feet. Then He told Satan his boundaries were still set. He could not touch Job's body.

"And the Lord said to Satan (the adversary and the accuser), Behold, all that he has is in your power, only upon the man himself put not forth your hand. So Satan went from

the presence of the Lord," and destroyed everything Job had, including his children (Job 1:12-19 AMP).

Job passed the test. He maintained his integrity and his faith in God, and *"sinned not nor charged God foolishly"* (Job 1:22). Not to be outdone, however, Satan decided to pay God another visit. The angels are once again gathered together before the presence of the Lord in Chapter 2 when in walks Satan, again accusing Job before God just as he had done in Job 1.

> *"Skin for skin!"* he said. *"Yes, all that a man has will he give for his life. But put forth Your hand now, and touch his bones and his flesh, and he will curse and renounce You to Your face"* (Job 2:4-5 AMP).

Satan's goal was to make Job curse God to His face, which to him would have been the ultimate victory—for the created to curse its Creator. God allowed Satan to plague Job with disease, but again, he set his boundaries and told him, *"Behold, he is in your hand; only spare his life"* (Job 2:6).

Although the devil succeeded in attacking Job and killing his children and destroying all of his earthly possessions, Job still did not bow the knee when Satan plagued his body with boils. He did not curse God, although his wife—frustrated and hurt by the loss of her children and their wealth—suggested he do so.

"So Satan went forth from the presence of the Lord and smote Job with loathsome and painful sores from the sole of his foot to the crown of his head… Then his wife said to him, Do you still hold fast your blameless uprightness? Renounce God and die!" (Job 2:7, 9 AMP)

Thank God that Job maintained his integrity and trust in Him. Though he was tried in a fiery furnace of affliction, he remained steadfast and came forth as pure gold. And God restored everything he had lost.

Open Doors

Why did Job go through this trial in the first place? Why did God give the devil permission to attack him? The answer is quite simple. There was an open door that the devil had legal access to; there was a gap in the wall or hedge that was supposed to protect Job and his family.

Job's hedge was breached long before Satan accused him. How? By fear. Job 3:25 says, *"For the thing which I greatly feared is come upon me, and that which I was afraid of is come unto me."*

Job feared that his children would sin before God during their days of "feasting" and curse or disown God in their hearts. This fear was so real to Job that he offered burnt offerings for them and atoned for their sins *every time* they had a feast.

69

*"And when the days of their feasting were over, Job sent for them to purify and hallow them, and rose up early in the morning and offered burnt offerings according to the number of them all. For Job said, It may be that my sons have sinned and cursed or disowned God in their hearts. Thus did Job at **all [such] times.**"* (Job 1:5 AMP)

You might think Job's behavior was proactive, but there was something about it that left a gap in his hedge of protection and allowed the enemy to come in and accuse him before God. Instead of taking the shield of faith referred to in Ephesians 6:16, which is able to extinguish every fiery dart of the devil, Job built a wall of fear around his children. Faith in God is impenetrable. Fear of the unseen is not. Therefore, Satan operated in his legal jurisdiction when he asked the Lord permission to breach the wall God had built around Job.

I know a woman who feared from her daughter's birth that she would become a lesbian. Though her fear was unfounded, it, among other things, drove her to be overprotective and to limit the girls she allowed her daughter to associate with. Needless to say, her daughter conformed to her mother's fears and became the person her mother feared she would be. Death and life are not only in the power of your tongue, but also in the power of your corresponding actions.

SPIRITUAL WARFARE

Ministering Spirits

A lot has been said about angels and angelic assistance in the lives of believers, so it would behoove us to take a look at the behind-the-scenes activity of this army of spirit beings.

The word *angel* means "messenger"; thus, angels may be described as God's messengers who carry out His will as they obey His commands (see Psalm 103:20). Angels can be seen throughout the Old and New Testaments; from Genesis to Revelation, the Bible is replete with angelic activity and divine visitations.

One of the first times we read about angels is in Genesis 3:24, when Adam and Eve were banished from the Garden of Eden. To ensure that man did not partake of the tree of life and live in a sinful state forever, God positioned angels to guard it day and night: *"So he drove out the man; and he placed at the east of the garden of Eden Cherubim, and a flaming sword which turned every way, to keep the way of the tree of life."*

Angels are spirits, created by God to help carry out His will in the earth, which is to save all mankind (see Psalms 103:20-21; Hebrews 1:14). They operate under delegated power and authority, as demons do, and are not to be worshipped.

Angels are likened unto fire, which is what they look like in the realm of the spirit (see Hebrews 1:7). This is also illustrated in II Kings 2:11, when God transported the

71

prophet Elijah to heaven via a fiery escort. Even the cloud that followed Israel by day, and the fire that protected them by night, was a host of God's warring and protecting angels.

Angelic Functions

There are different kinds or rankings of angels, including seraphim, cherubim, and archangels. Their roles are quite delineated.

The seraphim and cherubim can be seen around the throne of God, worshipping Him. Archangels, such as Gabriel, deliver messages directly from the Father, or (as in the case of Michael) do spiritual warfare in the heavenlies. For a better understanding of the role of angels in the life of mankind, read Isaiah 6:3; Daniel 10; Luke 1:11-20, 26-38; and Hebrews 1:6.

Angelic assignments can be divided into four categories:

+ First, to minister strength to the servants of God, as noted in Psalm 103:20 and Daniel 10 (see also I Kings 19:7; Matthew 4:11; and Luke 22:43).
+ Secondly, to do warfare against the powers of darkness as seen in Daniel 10:13 (see Acts 12:7; Jude 9; and Revelation 12:7-8).
+ Thirdly, to carry out the judgment of God (see Matthew 13:41-42; Acts 12:21-23; and the book of Revelation).

+ Lastly, to protect and guard, as noted in Genesis 3:24 (see also Exodus 37:9; Numbers 22:23-35; Psalms 91:11; and Matthew 18:10).

Angels Unawares

I would run out of pages if I enumerated the number of times angels appeared to Old and New Testament believers. Angels are all around us, even today, and they yet minister on the behalf of the heirs of salvation.

I am sure you know people who suspect they have seen an angel but who were not sure. Hebrews 13:2 says to *"Be not forgetful to entertain strangers: for thereby some have **entertained angels** unawares."*

A former truck driver once told me that he was driving through the Appalachian Mountains of Pennsylvania in the wee hours of the morning through dense fog and a heavy downpour. His rig skidded off the road and was tee-tering off the side of the mountain. To this day, he says he does not know why the truck did not go over the edge.

A man in a tow truck suddenly appeared. "Need some help?" the man yelled in a southern voice.

"Yes," was the trucker's quick reply.

I am sure you can guess the rest of the story. After pulling the man and his rig to safety, the tow truck driver disappeared as suddenly as he had appeared. There was no trace of him or his tow truck anywhere to be found.

I have seen two angels that I am aware of. One appeared in my bedroom in the form of light during a difficult time in my life. I had gotten out of the will of God and was in danger of derailing His purpose for my life. I heard the "sound" of the angel, which sounded like a quiet hum or a vibration as it entered my room. It came in quietly as I lay in bed. It stood momentarily, as though checking out my situation, and left as quietly as it had come.

The second appearance was at a ministry meeting as we prayed before the service began. I looked up and there was a massive—and I do mean *massive*—angel standing in the front of the room. He reminded me of a centurion soldier, although I have never seen one. He stood at attention, looking straight ahead, with his arms to his side and a staff in his right hand. His body went through the twelve- to fifteen-foot ceiling of the hotel conference room.

Although I believe I understand the appearance of the first angel, I am not sure why the Lord chose to reveal the presence of the second. Even as I think about it today, I wonder if it was God's way of showing me that His angels are standing guard over the work he has called me to do.

Living in the Spirit

Spiritual activity is taking place around you 24/7. You are surrounded by angelic and demonic activity even though you do not always see it. Some people have reported having visions and seeing into the spirit realm. However, many

Christians have never had this experience. Regardless, the realm of the spirit does exist, and wars and rumors of wars are being fought for the souls of nations, churches, families, and individuals.

Chapter 11

THE WEAPONS OF OUR WARFARE

"For the weapons of our warfare are not carnal, but mighty through God to the pulling down of strong holds; Casting down imaginations; and every high thing that exalteth itself against the knowledge of God, and bringing into captivity every thought to the obedience of Christ." (II Corinthians 10:4-5)

Fighting the devil in your own natural ability is like boxing with your own shadow. You need spiritual weapons to fight spiritual forces, and God has equipped you with spiritual weapons with which to effectively wage warfare through prayer.

These weapons include the name of Jesus, the blood of the Lamb, and the Word of God. You are to use these weapons as a skilled marksman under the direct supervision of the Holy Spirit.

Pulling Down Strongholds

You will lose every battle if you fight according to your flesh—that is, the realm of your five physical senses. The Apostle Paul was aware of this in II Corinthians 10:5, when he wrote that believers must use weapons that are mighty *through* God to the pulling down of Satan's strongholds.

A "stronghold" is best defined as a fortified place for defensive purposes. There are several types of strongholds, including religious, geographical, and personal. We will focus on personal strongholds in this chapter.

A personal stronghold is a "mindset" impregnated with hopelessness that causes you to accept as unchangeable something that is contrary to the Word of God. It is a cave in your soul (your mind, will, and emotions) where you can hide from the light of Christ and the power of the Word. The deeper you retreat into the cave, the darker it becomes.

Personal strongholds cannot be seen with the naked eye. They are erected in the realm of the spirit and lodged into your mind and emotions. An example of a personal stronghold could be telling yourself that your life will never get any better, even though the Bible promises a better day is coming (see Psalm 30:5 and Galatians 6:9).

The Battlefield is the Mind

Military personnel are trained to think a certain way and to respond to their officers' commands. Similarly, you joined the army of God when you became born again and you should be training your spirit to hear and obey His commands.

God is a Spirit, and you are a spirit being in human form; therefore, He does not communicate to your mind. He communicates to your spirit. How? In the form of words, pictures, and/or impressions. However, so does the devil. Therefore, it is imperative that you learn to recognize God's voice and the gentle nudging of the Holy Spirit.

God's voice is soft and quiet. When He speaks, His instructions are in accordance with the Bible. They will bring peace. The voice of the devil and/or his imps, on the other hand, brings fear, torment, and pressure. Everything he tells you will contradict the Word of God and create chaos and confusion.

The Process

I know people who do not know the voice of God, nor how to protect themselves against the enemy's mental onslaughts. They are tormented with suicidal or homicidal thoughts that will not go away. Some have thoughts of lust, anger, helplessness, and fear. Unfortunately, many of these people have acted upon these thoughts, reportedly feeling powerless to resist their urgings.

While counseling is an effective method by which to control what can ultimately develop into a stronghold, the

Bible says these thoughts can be "pulled down" or completely eradicated through prayer.

Spiritual warfare takes place in the mind. Whoever controls the mind controls the person and wins the battle. Just as there is a gestation period for the prayers that incubate in your spiritual womb, so it is with personal strongholds. They do not develop overnight, but instead fester over a period of time. Here's how:

> **Step 1** is a single thought, i.e., "You are ugly, worthless, and not fit to live. You should do the world a favor and kill yourself." Although irrational and unfounded, these thoughts will not go away and they begin to torment you.
> **Step 2** occurs when you begin to meditate upon these thoughts.
> **Step 3** takes place when you agree with, embrace, and accept these thoughts as true.
> **Steph 4** is the final and often fatal step when you begin to act upon these thoughts and they become a self-fulfilling prophecy.

Granted, some people are better able to dismiss such mental assaults, while some will only dismiss certain thoughts and entertain others. The important thing to note is that while these thoughts are real, they are *only thoughts*. They are imaginations that can be annihilated through prayer.

The name of Jesus, the Word of God, and the Blood of the Lamb give you the ability to cast down imaginations and the power of every thought that is contrary to the Bible, and to take every thought captive. Thoughts are taken "captive" when you make them submit to the authority of the Word. Thus, you *must* become a *student* of the Word. As you read the Bible, your mind will become renewed—changed—and your way of thinking and doing will begin to align itself with the Bible.

Romans 12:2 says to *"not be conformed to this world: but be ye* **transformed** *by the renewing of your mind."* One definition of the word *transformed* means "to change the nature, function, or condition of; to convert."

As you "renew" the spirit of your mind to the Word of God, He will begin to live in you and through you, thus changing you from the inside out. Your walk, talk, and thoughts will become new.

Second Corinthians 5:17 says, *"If any man be in Christ, he is a new creature: old things are passed away; behold, all things are become new."* You become that "new" creature, and the old ways of thinking and doing become obsolete.

I know a lady who was filled with anger most of her young adult life. When she gave her heart to Jesus, He began to change her as she daily communed with Him in prayer and the reading of His Word. She realized she had "become new" when she no longer responded in anger but in peace, love, and joy.

Being transformed by the renewing of your mind is a function of the Holy Spirit's work in your life. As He does in prayer, He will fill your mouth if you open it. He will teach you how to use the weapons of your warfare if you daily read the Word and seek Him in prayer.

Doers and Not Hearers Only

Part of the transformation process for mind renewal is predicated upon your obedience to the Word. The writer of the book of James admonishes believers to *"be ye doers of the word, and not hearers only"* (James 1:22).

He likens the person who only *hears* the Word with a casual ear—even if he is reading the Bible—but walks away from it and does not live it out, to *"a forgetful hearer"* who forgets he belongs to God and is governed by His Word. Thus, he leaves His presence and acts like a carnal Christian—or worse yet, like a heathen.

The difference between a "hearer" of the Word and a "doer" of the Word is as different as night and day. The one who "hears" the Word but does not "apply" it to his life will never change.

Perhaps you have heard the saying, "When he was baptized, he went down as a dry devil and came up as a wet one"? Well, such is the case for "hearers" only. But those who both hear *and* obey the Word are transformed and changed, thus reflecting the attributes of the Lord who dwells on the inside of them.

By renewing your mind, you will be transformed into the image of Christ. The transformation and renewal process is strengthened as you make quality decisions to not only hear, but also obey, the Word of God. You will then be in a position to not only pray for yourself, but to also intercede for others. Strongholds *will* come down for you and for the people, places, and things for which you pray.

Chapter 12

IN THE FULLNESS OF TIME

*"But when the fullness of the time was come,
God sent forth his Son." (Galatians 4:4)*

Do you know that when a plane is taxiing down the runway, it is too late for you to get off? If you have inadvertently gotten on the wrong plane, or are having a panic attack because you are afraid the plane is going to crash, you will have to dig in your heels and ride it out.

The life of an intercessor can be a lot like that plane ride. There may be times when you will want to vacate your prayer assignment and go to a far, distant place where nothing else exists except you and the wind that is blowing across the ocean at the beach.

You may also feel like a woman I once knew named Sandy, who was close to delivering her first child. It was one of the hottest summers on record and she was so big she could not get comfortable. She longed to have her body back. Sandy finally asked the doctor to give her a C-section, which he promptly refused.

There may be times in which you feel like you have been pregnant with prayer long enough. Like Jesus in the Garden of Gethsemane, you will ask God to "take this cup from me." However, an intercessor can never take a break. Once you answer the call to pray and become pregnant with the heart of God for intercession, prayer will be as the word was with Jeremiah—like burning fire shut up in your bones (Jeremiah 20:9). You will not be able *not* to pray.

A Matter of Life and Death

Psalm 121:4 says the Holy Spirit neither slumbers nor sleeps; therefore, your spirit will always be on-call to pray at a moment's notice. I have been awakened in the middle of the night with a burden to pray. Sometimes I have wrestled with the Lord and tossed and turned for a while because I did not want to get out of bed. Fortunately, however, God won and was able to express Himself through me through prayer and intercession.

I do know of instances in which the prayer warrior did not answer the call to pray. These instances ended in tragedy. Some people lost their lives and others were raped, mutilated, and abducted—all because someone refused to pray.

I remember bargaining with God one summer as He awakened me to arise and pray. I begged Him for just one more hour of sleep. Well, I do not know how much time had passed when I suddenly heard Him say, "I want to get up!"

Through the Eyes of Faith

Whether you are in your first trimester of prayer or at the point of giving birth, there is a due date for the delivery of the seed in your spiritual womb. It was twenty-one days for the prophet Daniel and twenty-five years for Abraham. I am still waiting for the answers to prayers that I prayed decades ago.

Some prayers will not be answered in your lifetime. They will be answered in the future, after you have gone home to be with the Lord. This is unfair, you might say. However, God is eternal and is not constrained by this thing we call "time." As He did with Abraham, He may use you to give birth to a promise that may take generations to fulfill.

For example, Abraham prayed to God for a son. God's answer was to give him nations. *"And he brought him forth abroad, and said, Look now toward heaven, and tell the **stars**, if thou be able to number them: and he said unto him, So shall thy seed be,"* (Genesis 15:5). You and your descendants are some of those "stars."

Abraham lived to see the birth of his son Isaac but he died before his seed multiplied and became as numerous as the stars in the sky. He did see the multiplication of his seed, however, with his spiritual eyes, through the eyes of faith. Hebrews 11:13 says, *"These all died in faith,* (including Abraham) *not having received the promises but having seen them afar off, and were persuaded of them, and embraced them."*

In the Fullness of Time

The realization that your prayers are just a tiny part of God's big, big picture can be humbling, especially when you understand that your responsibility is *only* to carry the baton until He says to pass it on to the next runner in the race.

I attended a conference in the late nineties where a well-known prophet was ministering. She told one of the attendees that God was still answering her parents' prayers. I was shocked because the woman's parents had died years ago; how could God be answering their prayers? Was the speaker a false prophet? The answer was "no."

Two things will remain on earth after you die—the souls you lead to the Lord and your prayers. So, the prayers of this lady's parents are still active and being answered, as are the prayers that have been prayed for you by the people who have gone home to glory. Even if you do not live to see the answers to what you have prayed, such as the nations and people that have incubated in your spiritual womb, know that God shall surely bring those answers to pass in the fullness of time when He is ready to make them manifest in the earth (see Galatians 4:4).

Set yourself to pray the price for people you may or may not know, or will never meet. Do as Paul instructed his son Timothy and *"endure hardness as a good soldier"* (II Timothy 2:3). And when you are at your lowest point and feel like turning in your intercessory prayer card, remember that there are seed in various stages of development incubating inside of your spiritual womb, just waiting for you to push them out through prayer.

CPSIA information can be obtained
at www.ICGtesting.com
Printed in the USA
BVHW070228310821
615478BV00002B/13